PIANO SOLOS

ISBN 978-0-6340-0388-2

Walt Disney Music Company
Wonderland Music Company, Inc.

DISTRIBUTED BY

HAL•LEONARD®
CORPORATION

7777 W. BLUEMOUND RD. P.O. BOX 13819 MILWAUKEE, WI 53213

Visit Hal Leonard Online at
www.halleonard.com

CONTENTS

Be Our Guest
from Walt Disney's BEAUTY AND THE BEAST

Lyrics by HOWARD ASHMAN
Music by ALAN MENKEN

Grandly

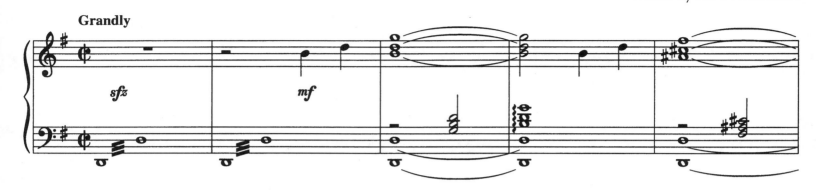

Moderate Showtune Tempo

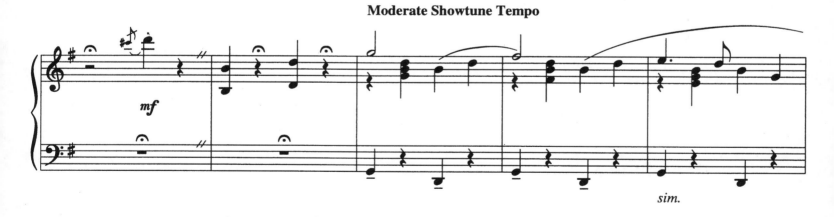

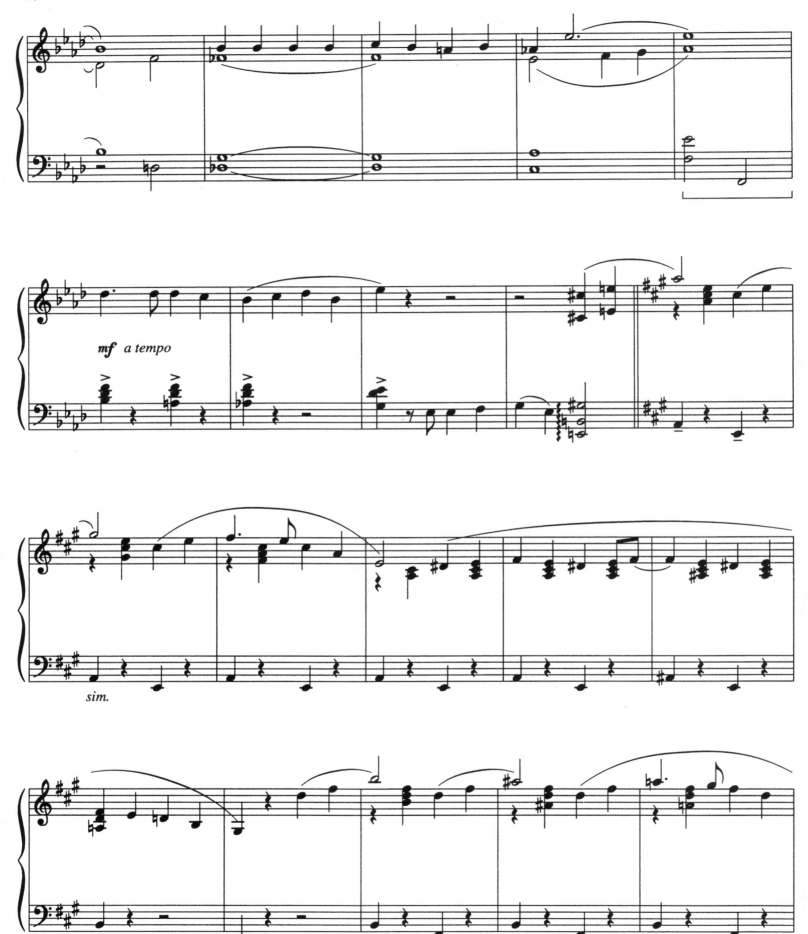

a tempo
ff

sim.

rit.

8va bassa

Chim Chim Cher-ee
from Walt Disney's MARY POPPINS

Words and Music by RICHARD M. SHERMAN
and ROBERT B. SHERMAN

rit.

a tempo

hold pedal to end

p

Can You Feel the Love Tonight

from Walt Disney Pictures' THE LION KING

Music by ELTON JOHN
Lyrics by TIM RICE

Freely and expressively

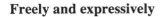

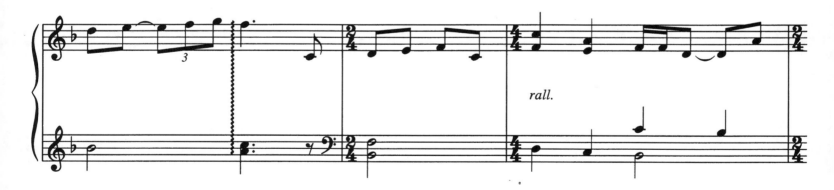

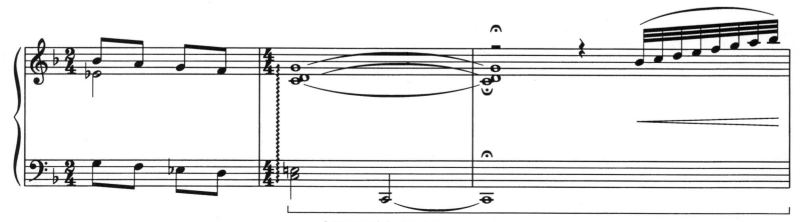

Moderately slow

Go the Distance
from Walt Disney Pictures' HERCULES

Music by ALAN MENKEN
Lyrics by DAVID ZIPPEL

Moderate Ballad

26

Kiss the Girl
from Walt Disney's THE LITTLE MERMAID

Lyrics by HOWARD ASHMAN
Music by ALAN MENKEN

With pedal

Hakuna Matata
from Walt Disney Pictures' THE LION KING

Music by ELTON JOHN
Lyrics by TIM RICE

Freely with soul

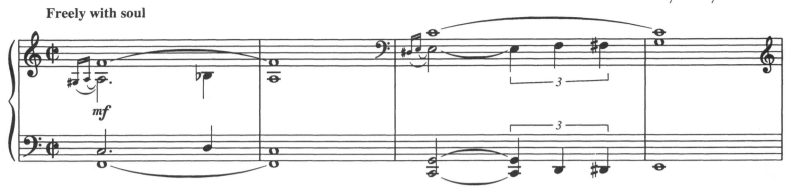

Bouncy shuffle (♫ = ♪ ♪)

35

36

If I Never Knew You

(Love Theme from POCAHONTAS)
from Walt Disney's POCAHONTAS

Music by ALAN MENKEN
Lyrics by STEPHEN SCHWARTZ

Moderately slow, expressively

With pedal

Love Will Find a Way

from Disney's THE LION KING II: SIMBA'S PRIDE

Lyrics by JACK FELDMAN
Music by TOM SNOW

Part of Your World

from Walt Disney's THE LITTLE MERMAID

Lyrics by HOWARD ASHMAN
Music by ALAN MENKEN

Moderately, somewhat rubato

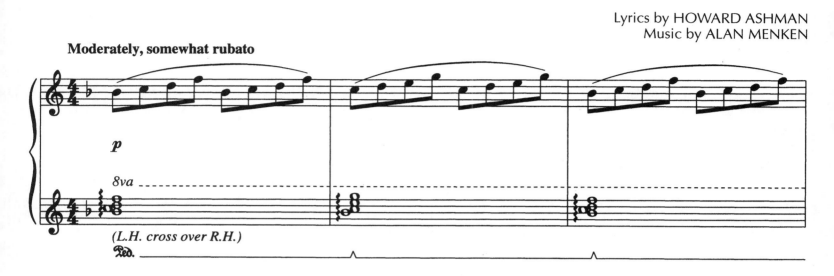

53

Reflection
from Walt Disney Pictures' MULAN

Music by MATTHEW WILDER
Lyrics by DAVID ZIPPEL

Moderately slow

62

To Coda $\oplus$

D.S. al Coda
(take 2nd ending)

CODA

rit.

mf *a tempo*

A Whole New World
from Walt Disney's ALADDIN

Music by ALAN MENKEN
Lyrics by TIM RICE

Someday
from Walt Disney's THE HUNCHBACK OF NOTRE DAME

Music by ALAN MENKEN
Lyrics by STEPHEN SCHWARTZ

Zip-A-Dee-Doo-Dah

from Walt Disney's SONG OF THE SOUTH

Words by RAY GILBERT
Music by ALLIE WRUBEL

Brightly, swing style

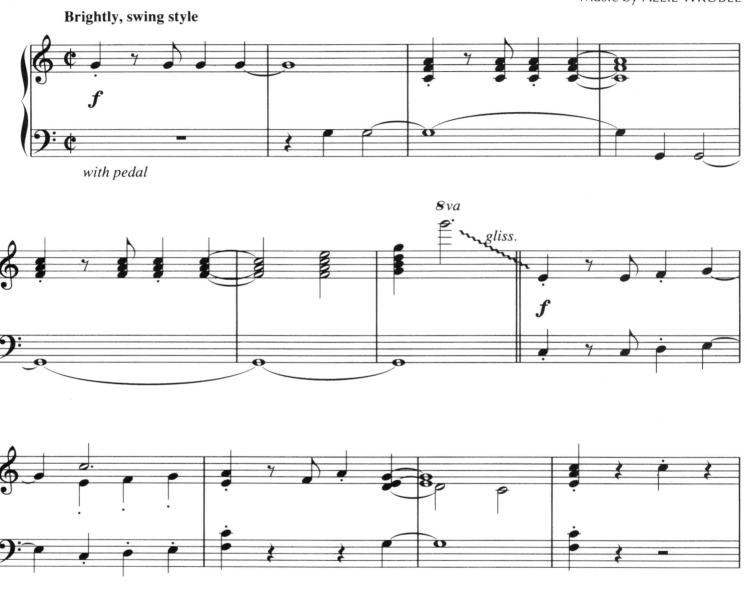

You've Got a Friend in Me

from Walt Disney's TOY STORY

Music and Lyrics by
RANDY NEWMAN